The Road To Hilo!
A Kid's Guide To Hilo, Hawaii

Photography by John D. Weigand
Poetry by Penelope Dyan

Bellissima Publishing, LLC
Jamul, California
www.bellissimapublishing.com

Copyright © 2013 by Penny D. Weigand and John D. Weigand

All rights reserved. No part of this book may be reproduced or transmitted in any form or by any means, electronic or mechanical, including photocopying, recording, or by any other means, or by any information or storage retrieval system, without permission from the publisher.

ISBN 978-1-61477-117-3
First Edition

There are only two mistakes one can make
along the road to truth;
not going all the way, and not starting.

Buddha

The Road To Hilo!
Bellissima Publishing, LLC

Introduction

Hilo, Hawaii is a city on the 'Big Island of Hawaii,' and the 'The Big Island' is still growing due to all the volcanic eruptions on the island, and if you go there you will see lots and lots of volcanic rock, but more than that you will see long roads and lots of bridges, if you know where to look for them. This book by the award winning author, attorney, vocalist and former teacher, Penelope Dyan, with photographs by John D. Weigand, is a kid's guide to Hilo, Hawaii; but like the other Dyan/Weigand travel books for kids, it isn't about things and places as much as it's about the feel of a place, and it is meant to help children develop reading skills though word recognition, repetition and rhyme, and to give kids something for them to contemplate. It is about seeing with the eyes, what most adults miss, and about asking the questions most adults never bother to ask. This book is the second of three books about 'The Big Island.' And these three books have extra large print for little eyes and are perfectly sized to be held by little hands, with just enough information in them so as not overwhelm a young child. There is also a music video that goes along with this book on the Bellissimavideo YouTube Channel that will further enhance the learning process as well as the fun; because if you don't have fun learning, you won't love to learn!

The Road To Hilo!
Bellissima Publishing, LLC

The Road To Hilo!
A Kid's Guide To Hilo, Hawaii

Photography by John D. Weigand
Poetry by Penelope Dyan

The road to Hilo isn't that far.
And you can see lots of things
from the window of your car.
You see dark lava and skies of blue,
and your mother reminds you,
that this island is YOUNG
just like YOU!
And like YOU (this much you know)
the Big Island of Hawaii
will CONTINUE to grow!
Volcanic eruptions create new land
as first fiery molten lava
becomes rock hard lava,
that slowly changes into sand.

You see a church
and you see a steeple.
You ask your dad,
"Where are all the people?"
It is just like
that funny finger game you play.
But there are no people
inside THIS church today!

Your dad decides to make a stop,
because your mother wants to shop.
She tells your dad she won't be long.
She wants to buy an Hawaiian sarong.

You see the ocean through the trees.
Outside there is a gentle breeze.

Hahai no ka ua i ka ulula'au.*
You stop and watch a waterfall,
a beautiful sight to see!
You gaze in wonder at the sight
of every flower and vine and tree.
This place is a rain-forest,
you are told,
more precious to the earth,
than silver or gold.

* Translation: The rain follows after the forest.
Meaning: Destroy the forest and the rain will cease.

And when you get to Hilo,
there the great
King Kamehameha stands.
(at Wailoa River State Park)
He's saluting Hawaii,
its people, and its lands.

You see a grand bridge,
the first of more to come.
And you run across
the soft green grass,
so happily in the sun.*

*This is also at Wailoa River State Park in Hilo.

Then . . . not so very far away,
you find another bridge
and another park
where you can play!*

*This is Liliuokalani Gardens & Waihonu Pond

Surprise! There is another bridge!
There are bridges all over this place!
You decide to cross
EVERY single bridge
built in this glorious place!
Your mother tells you no bridge
goes to nowhere,
even though it may seem so,
especially if it is to the OTHER side,
(of the bridge)
that you REALLY want to go!*

*This is also Liliuokalani Gardens & Waihonu Pond.

And then you see one MORE bridge!
It goes to a small island in the sun.
You tell your mom and dad
that you want to cross THAT bridge!
'Cuz it will be a lot of fun!*

* This is the bridge to Coconut Island Park.

And so you cross that bridge,
to get to the other side.
Because from the rest of the world
sometimes you want to hide.
You can relax and breathe in
the clean ocean air.
And you REALLY don't NEED
to go anywhere!

Your mother again reminds you
that a bridge to nowhere
still has somewhere to go,
even if you don't think that it's so.
Because some bridges play their part,
by simply being works of art!*

* This is Coconut Island Park.

"People are lonely because they build walls instead of bridges."

Author Unknown